Contents

Section	Page
Walk 1 - Wye	3
Walk 2 - Swarling	8
Walk 3 - Ickham	14
Guide to Wild Flowers	18
Guide to Trees	19
Guide to Fungi	20
Guide to Crops	21
Guide to Minibeasts	22
Guide to Pond and Stream Life	23
Guide to Freshwater Life	24
Guide to Waterfowl	25
Guide to Birds and Butterflies	26
Guide to The Rocky Shore	27
Walk 4 - Sandwich	28
Walk 5 - Perry Wood	35
More wild places	40
Wild about the Coast	42
Wordsearch and Scoring	44

Wild About East Kent

This book is dedicated to Archie and Bailey

The maps in this book are illustrative and are not necessarily drawn to scale. Every care has been taken in the production of this publication and the information was correct at the time of going to press. Wildside Guides and the author cannot accept responsibility for any injury, loss, damage or expense resulting from the use of the information contained in this book.

All rights reserved. No part of this publication may be reproduced, stored in a retrieval system or transmitted in any form or by any means, electronic, mechanical, photocopying, recording or otherwise, without the prior written permission of Wildside Guides.

This book has been written and illustrated by local artist Pamela Rees with the maps contributed by Simon Rees.

Published in the U.K. by Wildside Guides.

www.wildsideguides.co.uk

© Wildside Guides 2010   ISBN 978-0-9552769-2-7

email: info@wildsideguides.co.uk

Walk 1 - To the Wye Crown

Distance = 4km (2.5 miles)

Starting point
Drive through Wye, taking the road towards Hastingleigh and stop at the car park opposite the Devil's Kneading Trough.

1) From the car park, cross the road to some double gates opposite and enter the field.

2) Head diagonally across the field towards some hawthorn bushes and the top of the Devil's Kneading Trough.

How many different wildflowers can you see? - 10 points for each species spotted.

3) Cross the field and reach a gate that is the entrance to a nature reserve. Do not enter here but turn right and follow the fence up to another gate.

4) Pass through this gate and then continue to follow the path with woodland on your left.

5) Head into the woods, following the path between two posts with green nature trail signs on them.

Total points

Did Woolly Mammoths walk on these hills?

Woolly mammoths, woolly rhinoceros, reindeer and wild horses were able to survive the harsh cold climate of the Ice Age. Kent was on the edge of the ice sheet during the last Ice Age and, over 15,000 years ago, as the temperature rose the melt waters carved deep channels in the chalk uplands.

This has left steep and fascinating valleys on the edges of the Downs. The Devil's Kneading Trough is one of the best examples of this. Fossilised remains of the animals have been found where the waters drained away towards the sea.

The chalk uplands were formed over 65 million years ago when most of Britain was under the sea, Chalk is made up of the shell like remains of tiny plants and animals. Other, much older fossils, can be found in the chalk, such as sea-urchins, ammonites, fish and reptiles.

6) Follow the path through the woodland until you reach the road.

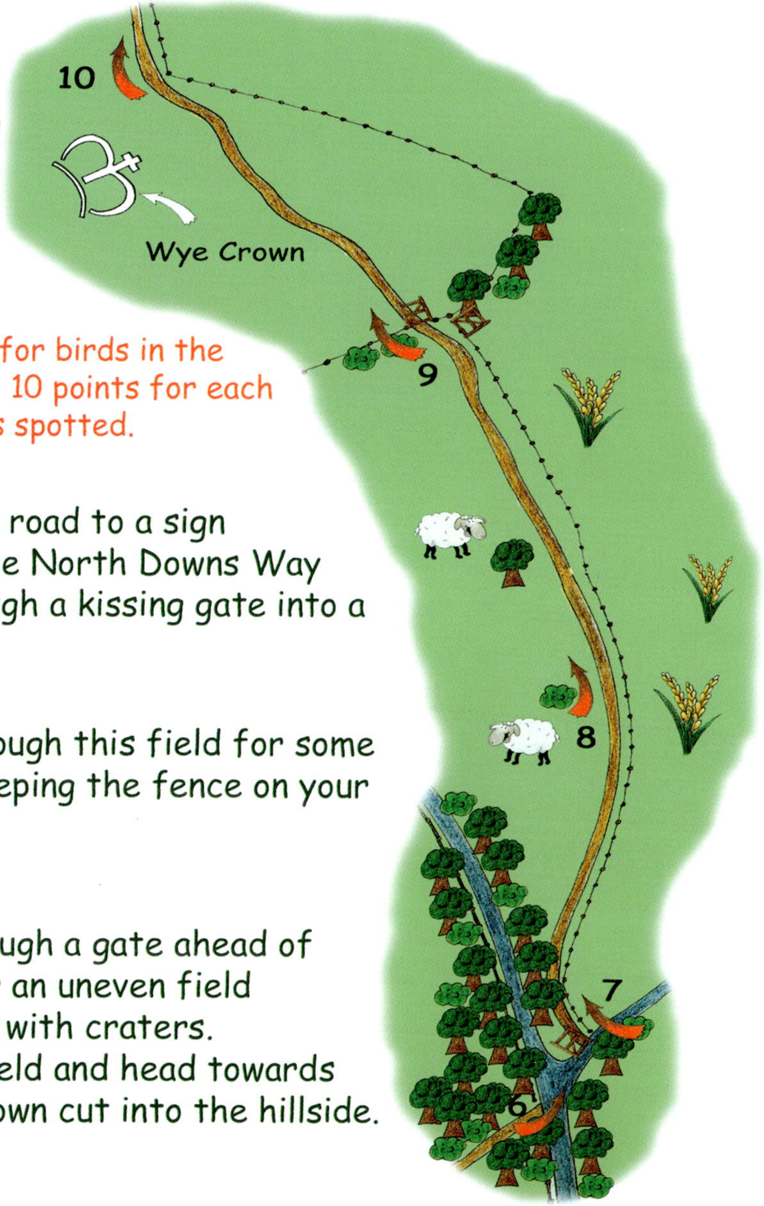

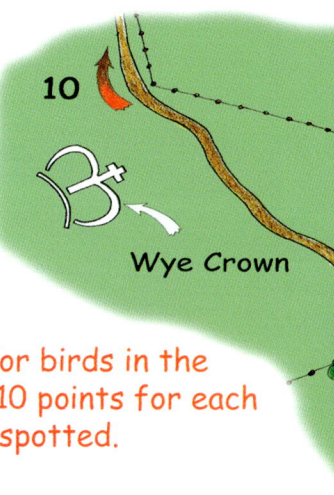

Listen for birds in the trees - 10 points for each species spotted.

7) Cross the road to a sign indicating the North Downs Way and go through a kissing gate into a field.

8) Walk through this field for some distance, keeping the fence on your right.

9) Pass through a gate ahead of you to enter an uneven field pockmarked with craters. Cross the field and head towards the Wye Crown cut into the hillside.

10) Upon leaving the crown, follow the edge of the fence and walk towards the woods ahead of you.

Total points

5

11) Ignore the stile ahead of you and, instead, turn right through a small "squeeze" gate and follow the path between the woods and a ploughed field.

20 points if you can identify the crops in the field - use your guide on page 21 to help you.

12) Turn right on to a lane and walk up the hill.

13) When the lane turns to the left, continue ahead, on the farm track labelled "by-way".

Can you identify the fruit trees in the orchard - 10 points.

14) As this track bends to the left, take the grassy track ahead of you.

Total points

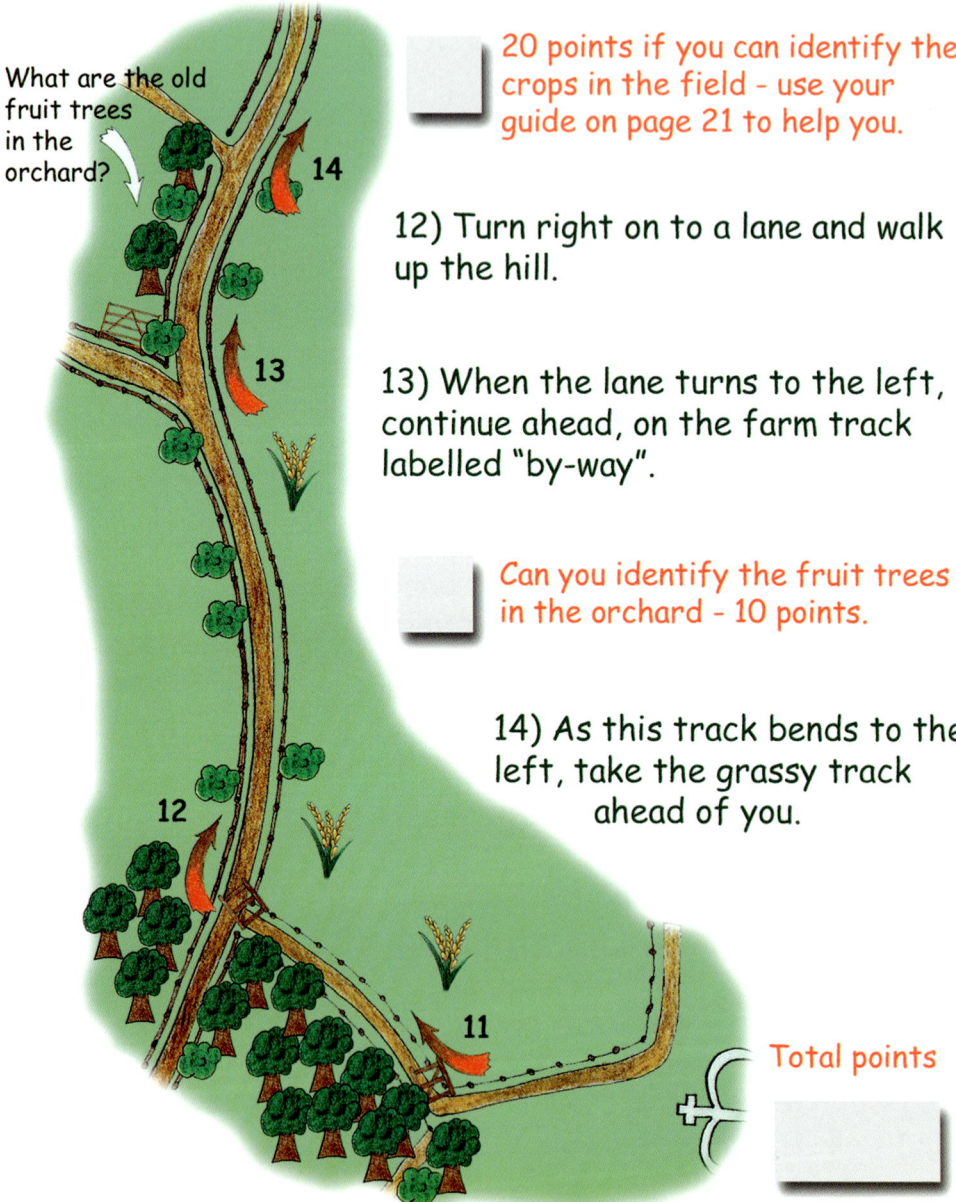

What are the old fruit trees in the orchard?

15) Go through a gate ahead of you and then, almost immediately, turn right to enter the field through a small gate.

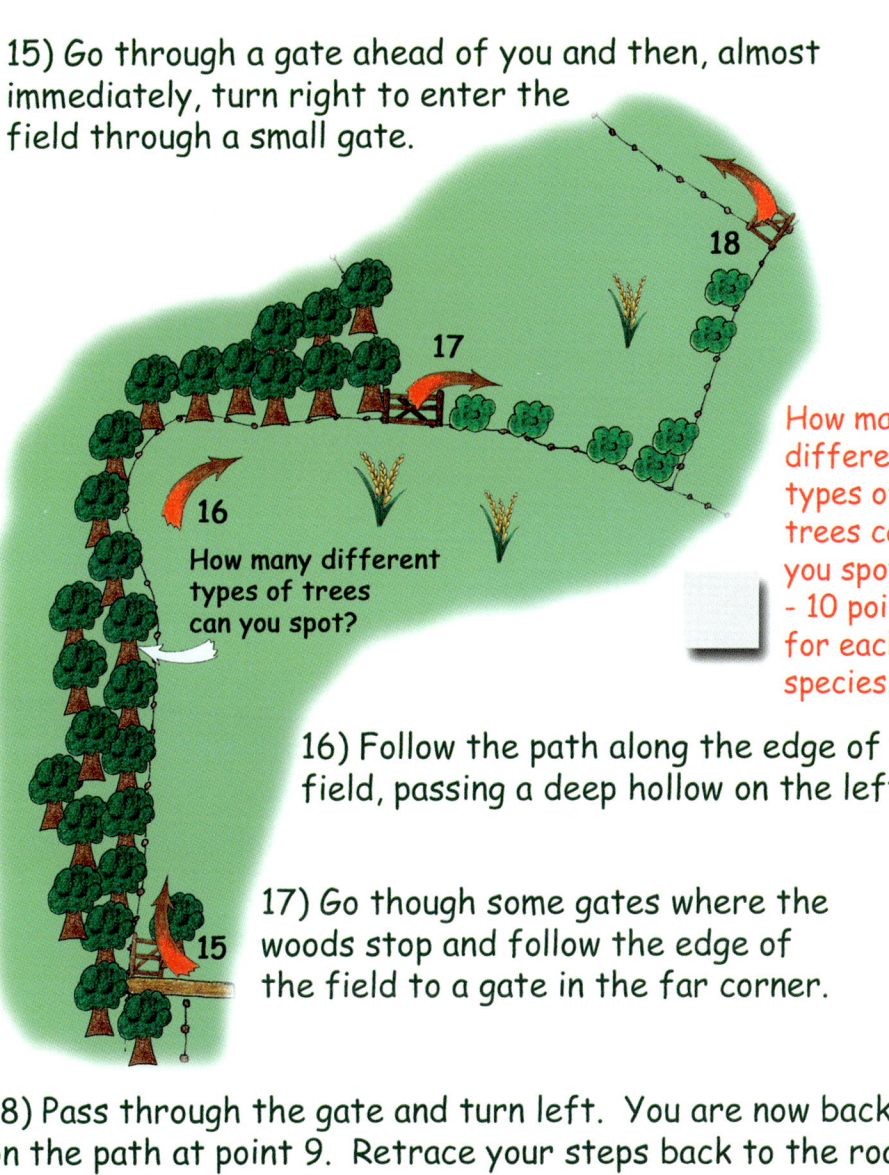

How many different types of trees can you spot?

How many different types of trees can you spot - 10 points for each species.

16) Follow the path along the edge of the field, passing a deep hollow on the left.

17) Go though some gates where the woods stop and follow the edge of the field to a gate in the far corner.

18) Pass through the gate and turn left. You are now back on the path at point 9. Retrace your steps back to the road and then the car park.

On the way back, can you spot a creature or plant for each letter of the alphabet? e.g. A for ant, B for beetle.... - 5 points for each one.

Total points

Walk 2 - Swarling

Distance = 4km (2.5 miles)

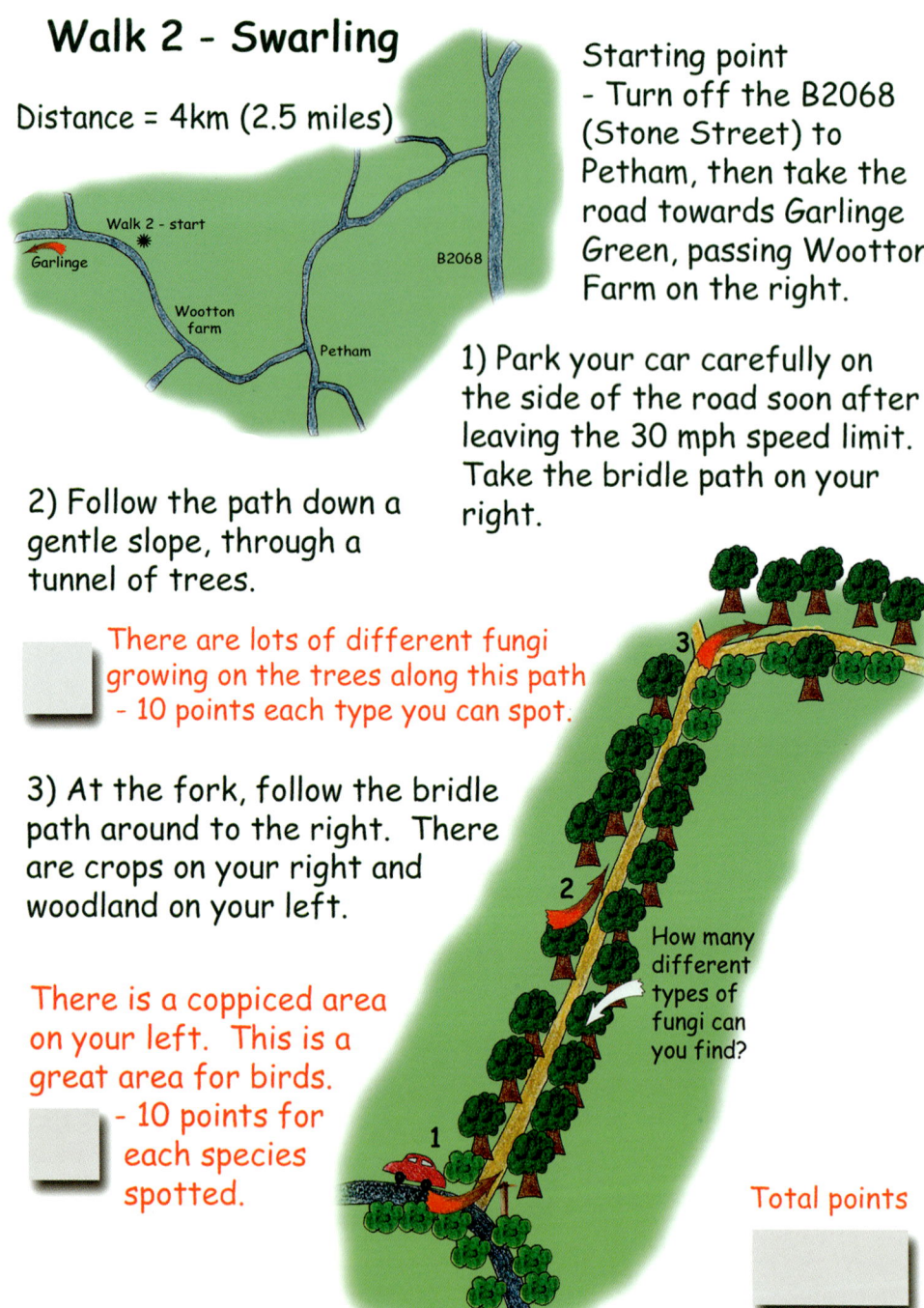

Starting point - Turn off the B2068 (Stone Street) to Petham, then take the road towards Garlinge Green, passing Wootton Farm on the right.

1) Park your car carefully on the side of the road soon after leaving the 30 mph speed limit. Take the bridle path on your right.

2) Follow the path down a gentle slope, through a tunnel of trees.

There are lots of different fungi growing on the trees along this path - 10 points each type you can spot.

3) At the fork, follow the bridle path around to the right. There are crops on your right and woodland on your left.

There is a coppiced area on your left. This is a great area for birds.
- 10 points for each species spotted.

How many different types of fungi can you find?

Total points

8

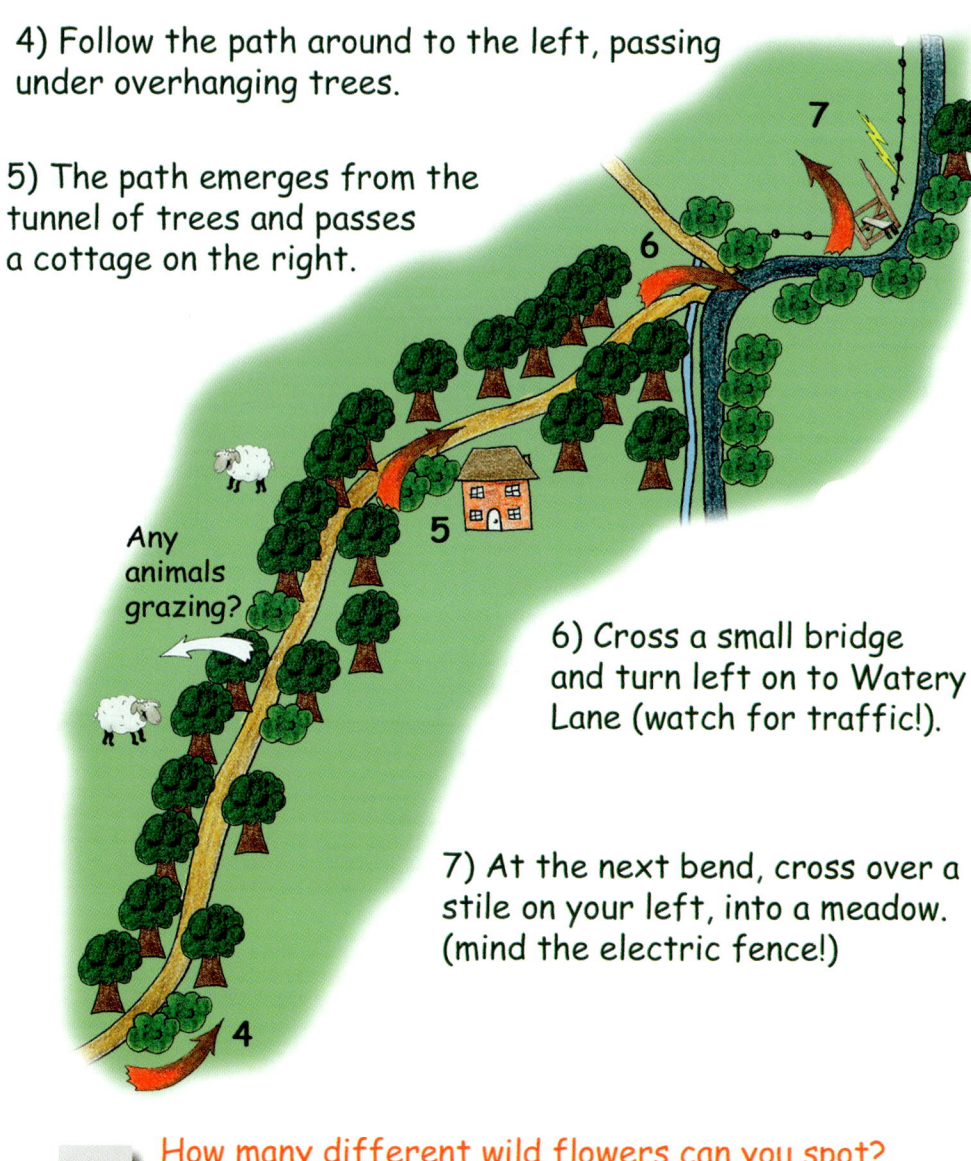

4) Follow the path around to the left, passing under overhanging trees.

5) The path emerges from the tunnel of trees and passes a cottage on the right.

Any animals grazing?

6) Cross a small bridge and turn left on to Watery Lane (watch for traffic!).

7) At the next bend, cross over a stile on your left, into a meadow. (mind the electric fence!)

How many different wild flowers can you spot?
- 10 points for each type
(use your guide on page 18 to help you).

Total points

The Garden of England

It is thought that Henry the Eighth named Kent "The Garden of England" after he established cherry and apple orchards around Teynham, near Faversham. At about the same time, hop gardens were developed.

The female hop flowers were harvested for adding to ale to make beer. The hop flowers had to be dried and Oast houses were developed. The distinctive square or round oasts with conical roofs topped by white cowls are a familiar site in Kent.

On the ground floor of the oast a smouldering fire of charcoal created heat. This hot air was drawn up by the revolving cowl to dry the hop flowers that were laid on a slatted floor above. Once golden and dried they were moved to a cooling room before being bagged and sent to the brewery.

Hop flowers

Less hops are grown now, but in the winter and spring you can still see hop gardens with rows of tall slanting poles wired together. Strings are added from the high wires to the ground for the hop bines to grow up from the crowns at their base. In September, the strings are cut to allow the bines to be collected and the flowers stripped from the plant. Modern drying methods now mean that the oast houses are mostly used as homes.

8) Leave the field by another stile and then walk through the farmyard with an Oast house on your left and a deep pond on your right.

Can you see any ducks?
 - 5 points for each one spotted

30 points for a heron

9) Turn left to follow the path between a high hedge and a metal fence.

10) Follow this path straight along, past Swarling Manor, crossing a small footbridge.

11) At the end of this path, cross over a stile and turn right into a marshy meadow. Stay on this path, ignoring a track going up the hill.

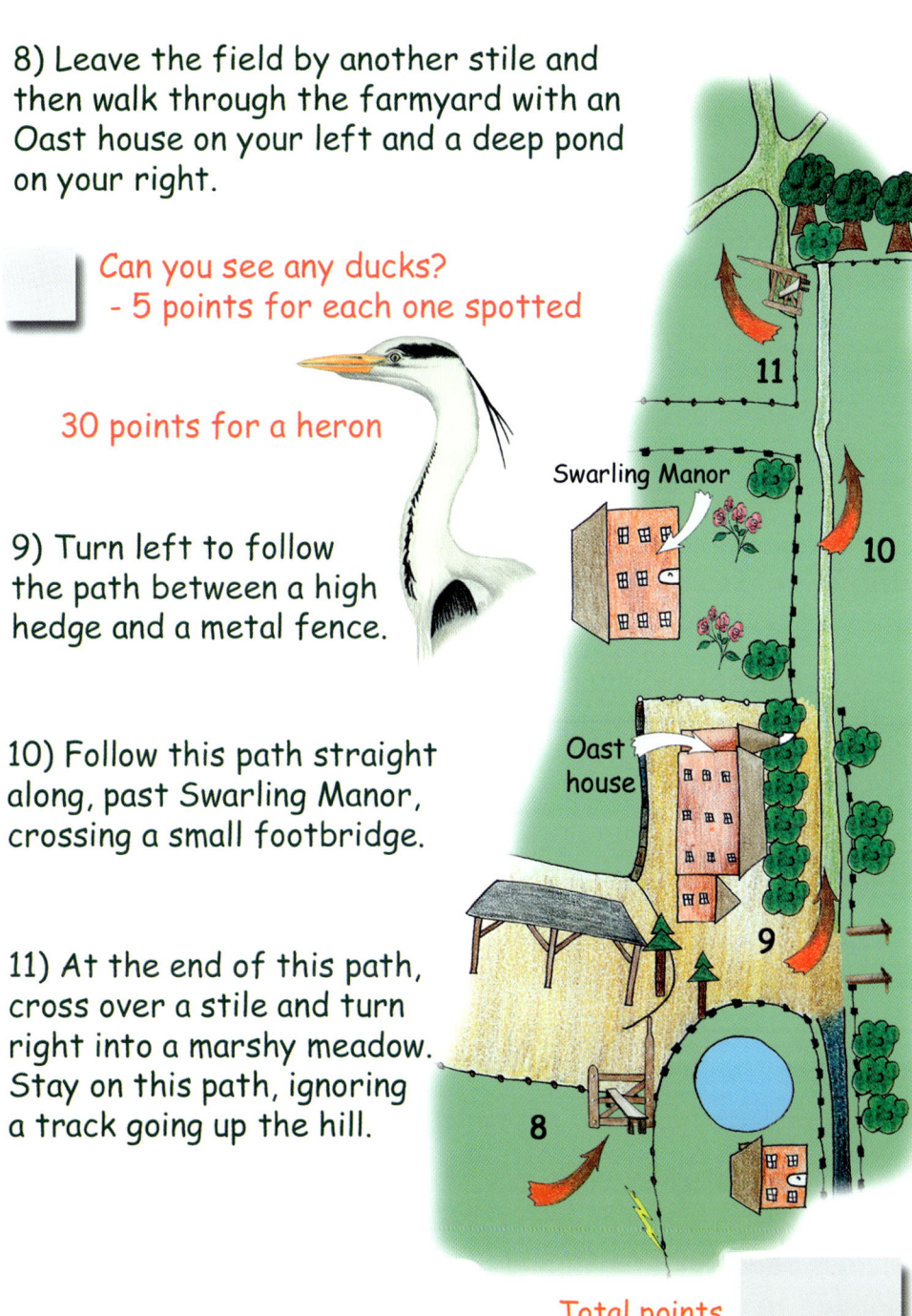

Total points

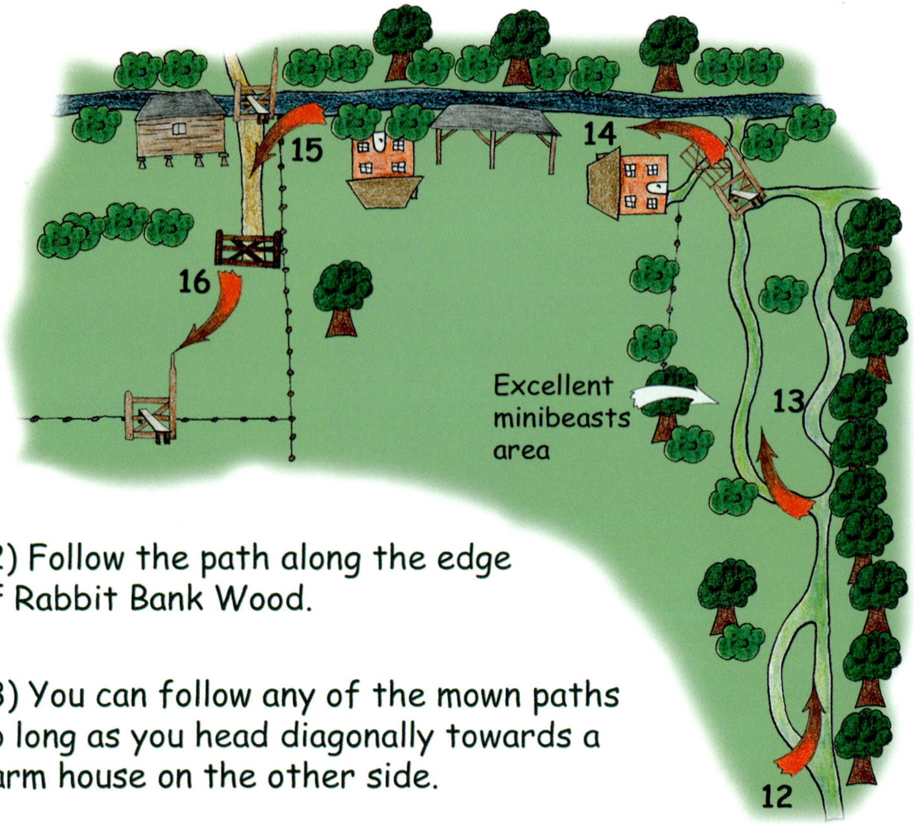

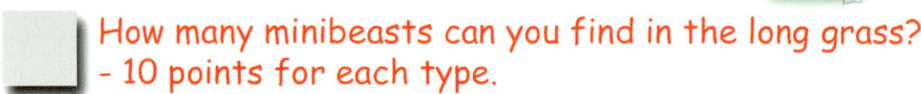

12) Follow the path along the edge of Rabbit Bank Wood.

13) You can follow any of the mown paths so long as you head diagonally towards a farm house on the other side.

How many minibeasts can you find in the long grass? - 10 points for each type.

14) Cross over the stile and then turn left at the road.

15) Walk along the road until you reach a stile on your left beside a granary on raised mushroom (Staddle) stones.

Why do you think the granary is raised off the ground? - 10 points for the correct answer.
(see bottom of the page)

16) Pass through a gate and across a garden to another stile.

Total points

Answer: to keep the rats and mice out!

12

17) Climb over the stile into open pasture and walk up the slope to your right, towards another stile.

18) Go over this stile into another area of pasture. Head for a small post with yellow markings on it and then a stile on the other side of the field

How many different trees can you spot? - 10 points for each type.

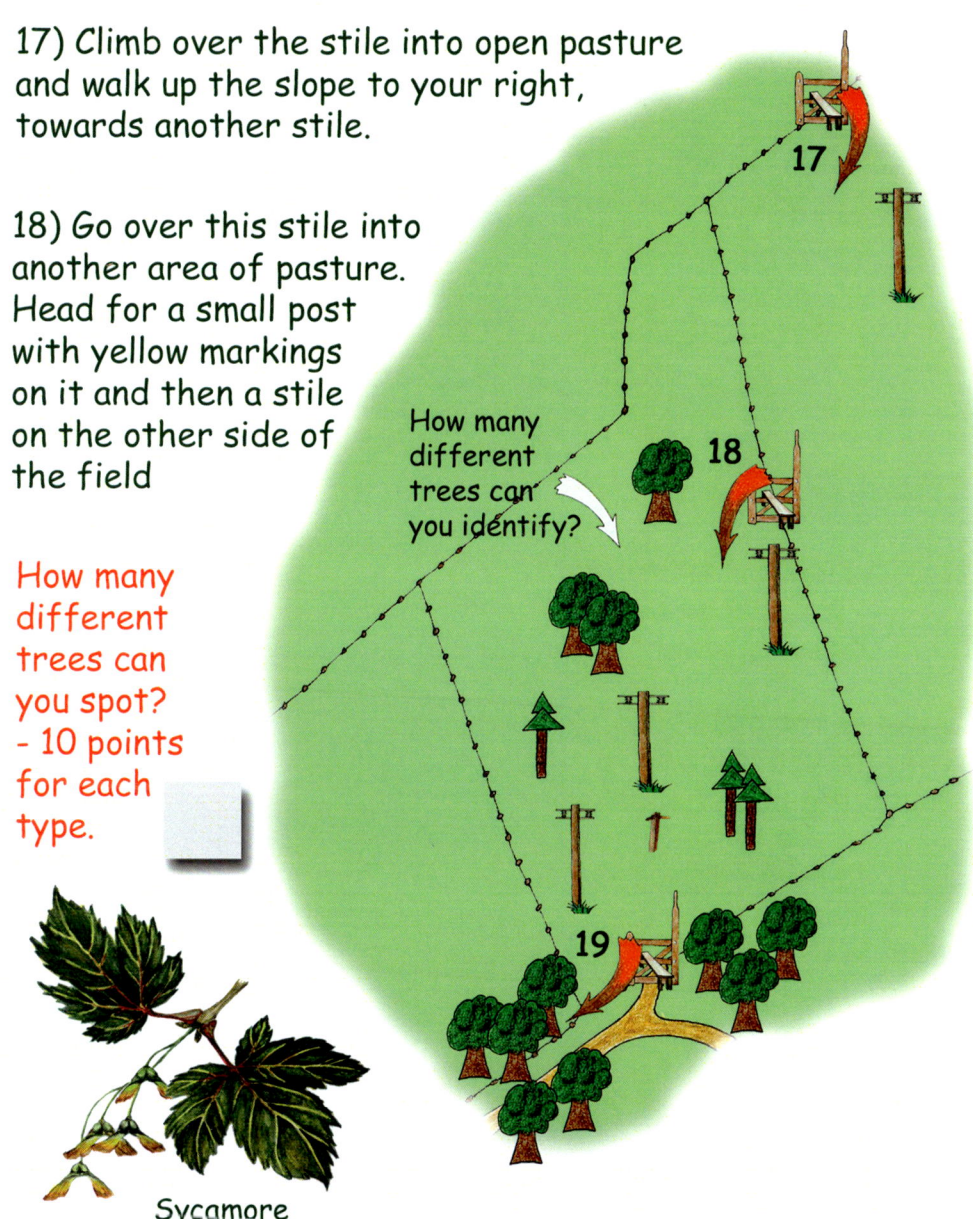

Sycamore

19) Climb over this stile and then turn right to head up the bridlepath and back to the start.

Total points

13

Walk 3 - Ickham

Distance = 3.25km (2 miles)
Starting point - Opposite the Duke William public house.

This is reached by turning off the A257 at Littlebourne, towards Wickhambreaux and then turning right to Ickham.

1) Park your car opposite the Duke William pub and go along the road to walk down the path towards the church.

2) Leave the main path to follow the footpath that curves to the right around the churchyard wall.

 10 points if you can identify the crops in these fields

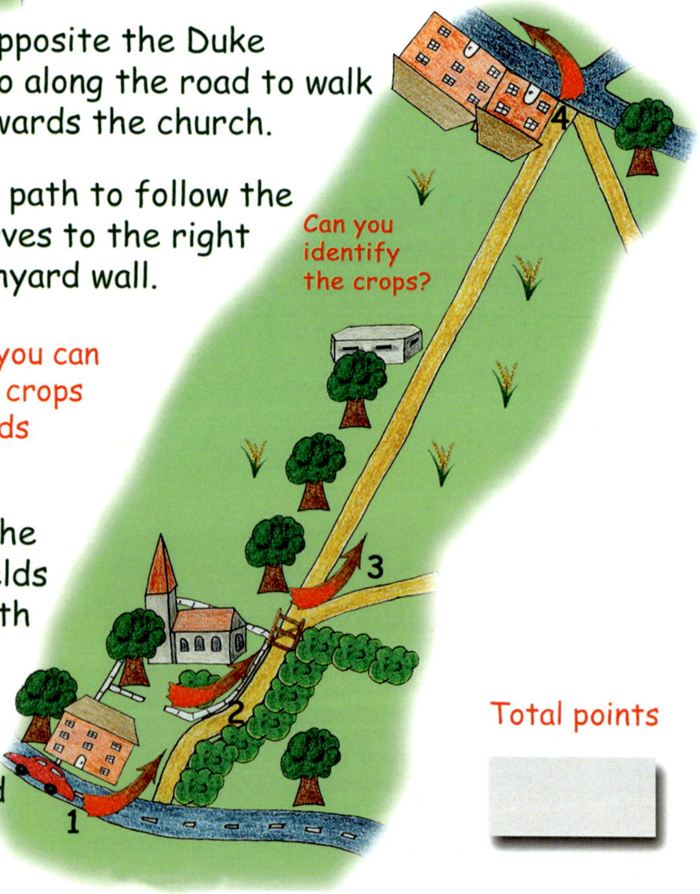

3) Pass through the gate into crop fields and follow the path straight ahead.

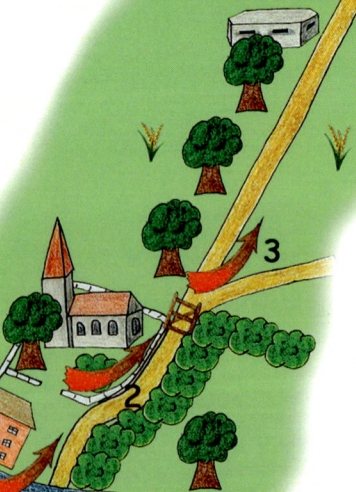

Can you identify the crops?

4) Cross the field and turn left at the road.

Total points

When the sky was full of more than birds

Only ten minutes flying time from the French coast, East Kent saw much of the Battle of Britain in the late summer of 1940. Try to imagine the Spitfires and Hurricanes droning overhead as you go on your walk through these now peaceful fields.

On the ground the Land Army girls would have been ploughing and harvesting, often using horses to save petrol for the aeroplanes. You can see these planes and learn about the battle at museums in Manston and Hawkinge.

Other reminders of wartime can still be seen alongside the footpaths. Concrete "pillboxes" were built as a string of small defensive forts across the whole country, usually near road junctions, rivers or canals. They provided cover for soldiers on look-out duty, usually armed with just one machine gun.

5) Go over the river by Seaton Mill and then cross over the stile on your left.

50 points if you see a kingfisher along the riverbank.

6) Follow the path straight ahead, which runs beside the stream, and then cross the field towards a stile.

7) At the road, turn left to follow the road in to the centre of Wickhambreaux, take your time to explore some of the old buildings here.

10 points if you can see fish in the river beside the Mill.

Perch

8) Go through a kissing gate into the churchyard. Follow the left hand edge of the churchyard and walk out behind Wickhambreaux Mill.

Total points

16

9) Follow the path straight along beside the river.

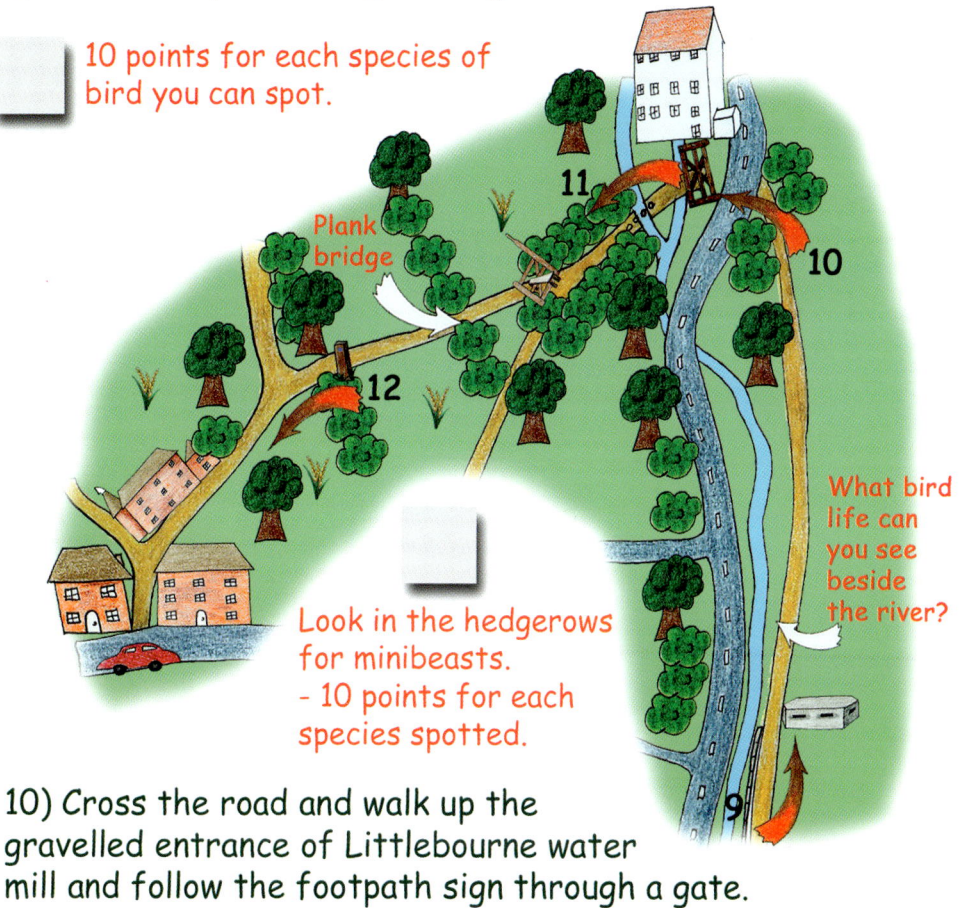

10 points for each species of bird you can spot.

Plank bridge

Look in the hedgerows for minibeasts.
- 10 points for each species spotted.

What bird life can you see beside the river?

10) Cross the road and walk up the gravelled entrance of Littlebourne water mill and follow the footpath sign through a gate.

11) Walk over the stepping stones and across a small field, following a narrow footpath between two high hedges. Cross the stile and walk across the meadow to a gap in the hedge with a plank bridge.

12) Head for a gap in the next hedgerow beside a large oak tree. Walk towards the oast houses and then follow the path back to the road.

Total points

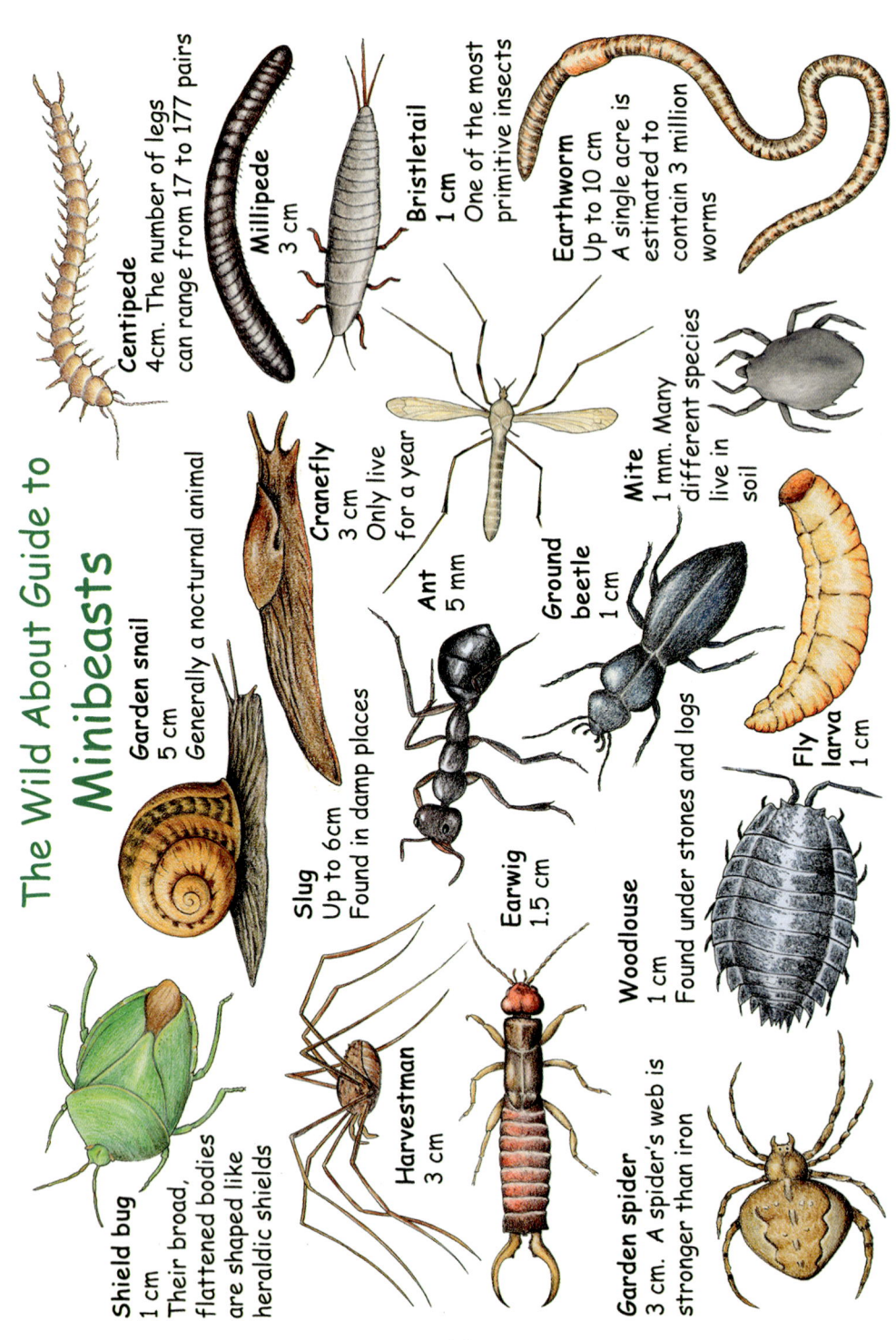

# Walk 4 - Sandwich
Distance = 3.5km
(2.25 miles)
Starting point
- Car park on the Quay

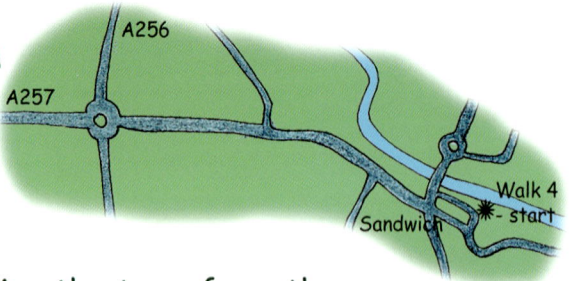

This is reached by entering the town from the A257 and heading to the large car park beside the river.

1) Walk from the car park with the river on your left and the road on your right. You should pass through a wooden gate adjacent to a slipway and then follow the path through a line of trees.

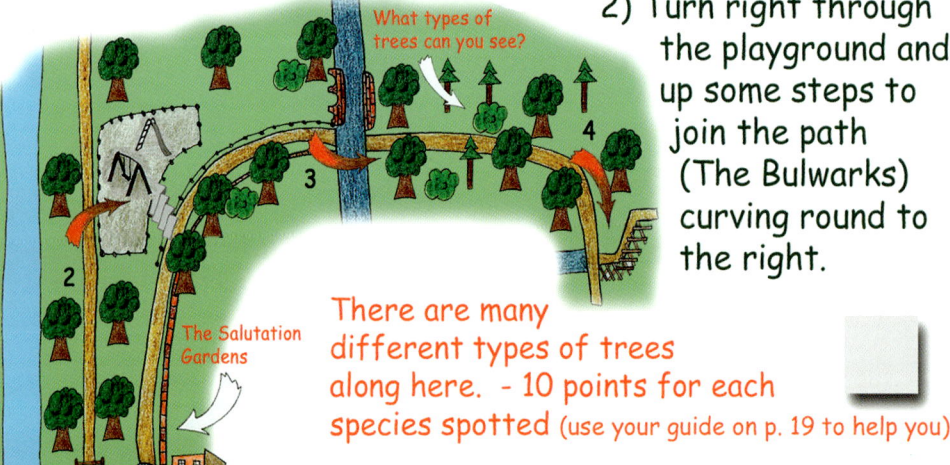

What types of trees can you see?

The Salutation Gardens

2) Turn right through the playground and up some steps to join the path (The Bulwarks) curving round to the right.

There are many different types of trees along here. - 10 points for each species spotted (use your guide on p. 19 to help you).

3) Cross the road and continue along the path (Mill Wall) directly ahead of you. There is now quite a steep bank on your left.

4) Follow the path round, passing a path on your left and "Knightrider Street" on your right.

Total points

28

5) Continue to follow the path until you reach a road.

6) Cross over the road and continue straight on along the Rope Walk.

Ramshorn snail

Try some stream dipping along here - 10 points for each species caught.

7) After some distance, cross another road and continue to follow the path (The Butts) beside the river.

What do you call a fish with 3 eyes? - a fiiish!!

Is there anyone fishing ? - 5 points for each fisherman spotted.

Total points

Bond, boats and battles

Ian Fleming played golf at Sandwich and he made James Bond meet Goldfinger on a golf course known to be based on the Royal St George's Golf Course at Sandwich. This was only possible because the sea has deposited sand and shingle over many years to form the "links" where the golf course was built. When the Romans built a fort at Richborough near the site of present day Sandwich, the sea came over the surrounding marshes.

By the time of the Battle of Hastings in 1066, Sandwich had become an important port. This made the town wealthy and it was frequently raided by the Vikings and the French. Notably, in 1457, the town was attacked by 4,000 Frenchmen. The citizens fought desperately all day until help arrived from the other Cinque Port towns. The Mayor of Sandwich was killed along with many citizens. In memory of this event, the Mayor of Sandwich still wears a black robe for ceremonial events. Although the importance of the port declined, in the First World War it again became an important embarkation point for troops and supplies.

8) Continue straight along the path, passing a cricket pitch on your left.

9) Cross the road and pass through a gate to join a path leading to the Gazen Salts nature reserve.

With the stream on your right and rough ground on your left, this is a good area for dragonflies in the summer - 10 points for any spotted.

10) After following the path round to the right, turn left to enter the nature reserve.

10 points for each type of bird you spot as you walk through the nature reserve.

Greater Spotted Woodpecker

11) Follow the path straight on, with the stream on your right. Ignore any paths to the left

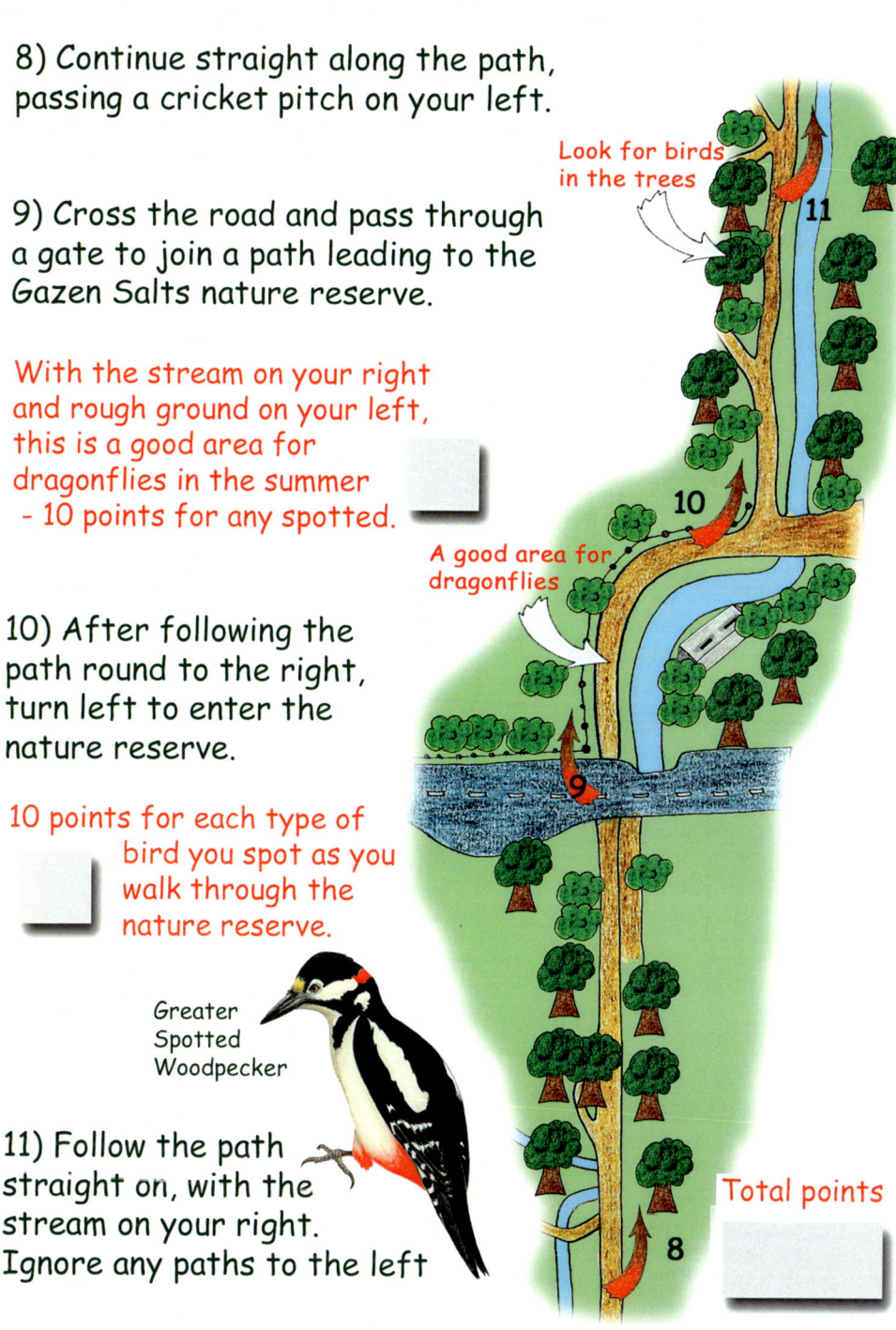

Look for birds in the trees

A good area for dragonflies

Total points

31

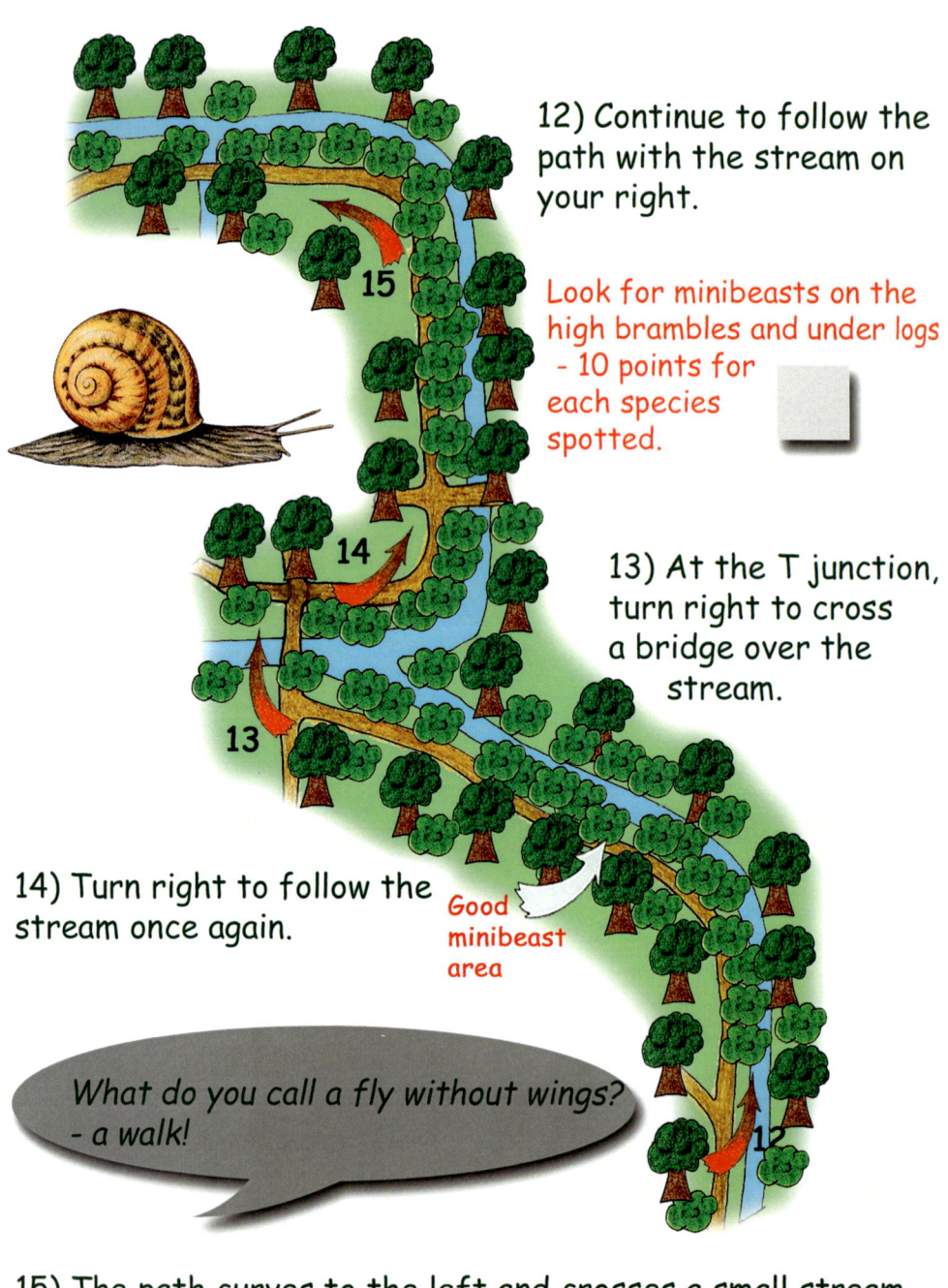

12) Continue to follow the path with the stream on your right.

Look for minibeasts on the high brambles and under logs - 10 points for each species spotted.

13) At the T junction, turn right to cross a bridge over the stream.

14) Turn right to follow the stream once again.

Good minibeast area

What do you call a fly without wings? - a walk!

15) The path curves to the left and crosses a small stream.

Total points

32

16) Take the second turning on the right that joins a path from the left to reach the lakeside.

How many different types of waterfowl can you spot? - 10 points for each species.

17) With your back to the lake, take the path to your left that leads away from the lake.

Try feeding the fish as well as the ducks!

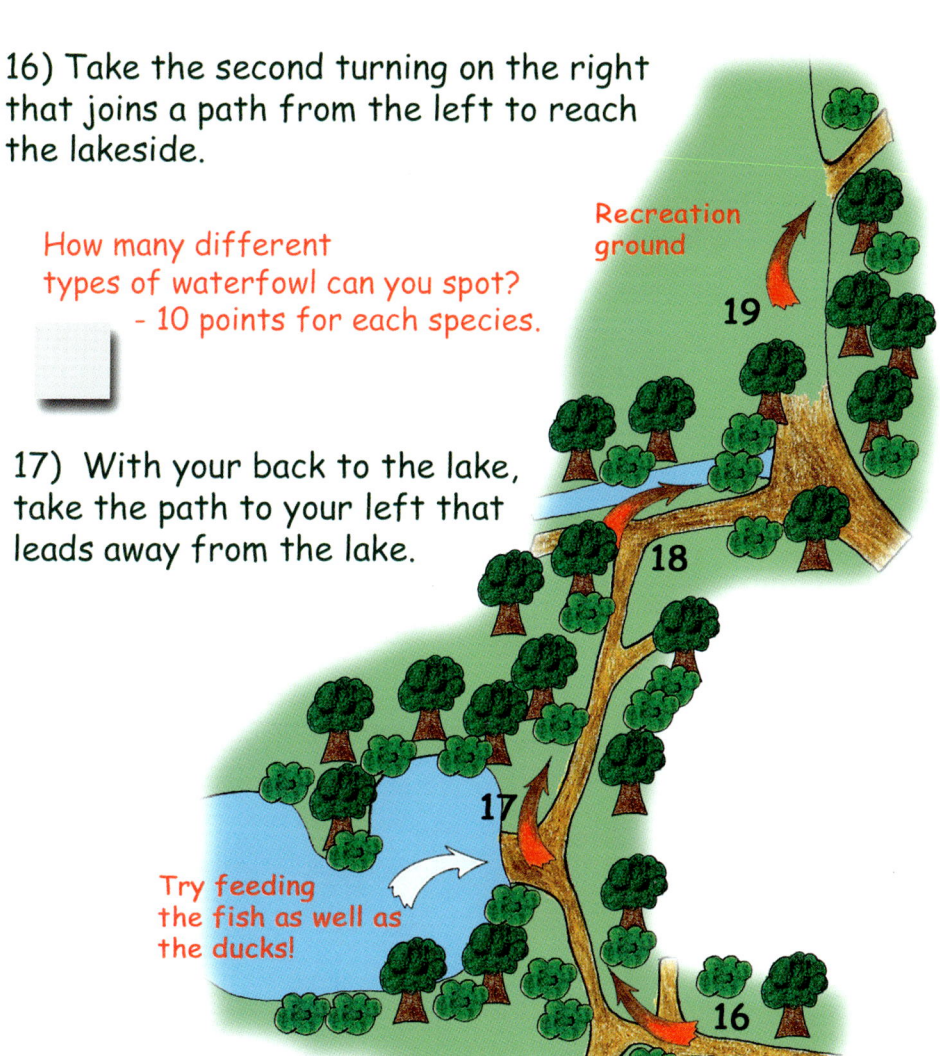

18) Turn right when you reach the path running along by the stream to return to the entrance to the nature reserve.

19) Turn left to walk along the edge of the recreation ground and then right down a path through the trees.

Total points

20) Follow the path to a gate and turn right on to a lane.

21) Turn left to follow the road through the town.

22) Turn left into a narrow lane that takes you down to the waterfront.

Which types of boat can you spot?

How many different types of boat can you spot?
- 5 points for each type.

10 points for each species of bird you can spot on the river.

23) Take care crossing the road beside the bridge and then walk back to the car park.

Total points

34

Walk 5 - Perry Wood

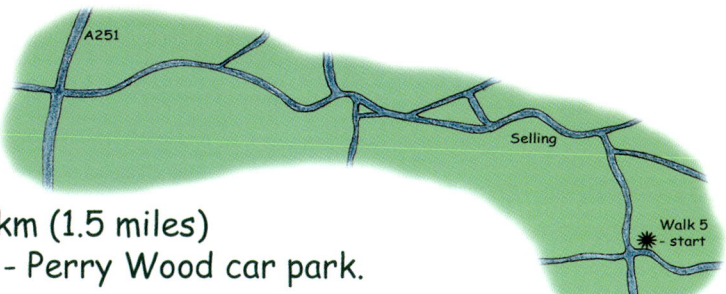

Distance = 2.5km (1.5 miles)
Starting point - Perry Wood car park.

This is reached by turning off the A251 to Selling and then turning right to Perry Wood after the village boundary.

1) From the car park, cross the road to a signposted bridleway.

2) Follow the path up the hill.

These woods are great for squirrels and other small mammals. - 20 points for any you spot or any evidence such as tracks or chewed pine cones.

3) Then pass a blue signpost and walk over some planks to reach an intersection of paths.

There are three carved signs on this section. Write the names here.

4) Take the path opposite that leads up a steep hill.

Total points

5) As you go up the hill, you will see another blue sign on your left. Follow the path round to the right.

6) Continue along the ridge, ignoring any paths on the right.

How many different types of trees can you identify? - 10 points for each type spotted.

7) At the lookout post, take the path that leads away down the hill past two more blue signposts.

How many different trees can you spot?

There are three more carved signs on this section.
Write the names here.

8) Head down the hill.

10 points if you can find the smooth pebbles along the path here. These form the "Oldhaven beds" and were left behind after the last ice age.

Steps

Total points

36

How to draw.... a badger.

This shy inhabitant of our woodlands emerges generally at dusk and is active at night. Large badger setts are the most obvious evidence of their presence.

Follow these steps to produce your own badger picture....

Step 1 - Draw an egg shape lying on its side for the body and a V shape for the head.

Step 2 - Draw in the nose and outline with a ruffled edge for the fur. Mark out the areas of white banding

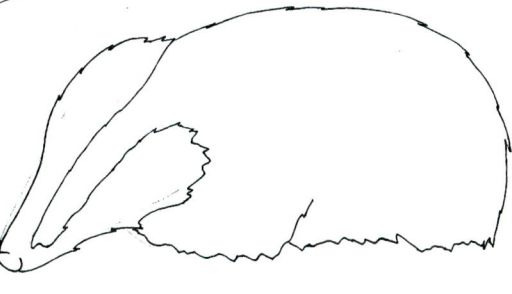

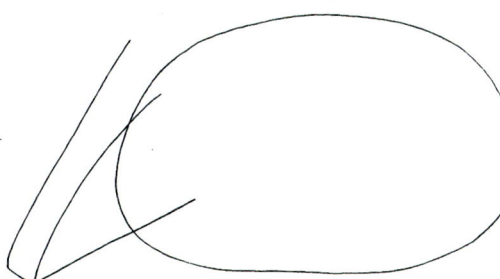

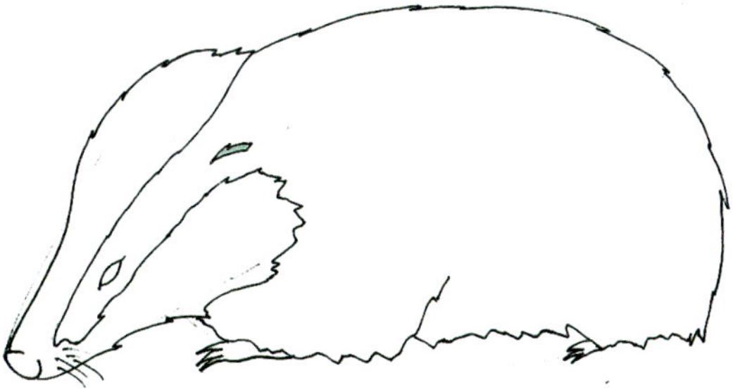

Step 3 - Draw in the eye, ear tuft and feet.

Step 4 - Colour in.
Try to use shading to give a 3 dimensional effect and leave a clear spot in the eye. Try adding some leaves and branches as well.

9) At the bottom of the hill, turn right.

How many wildflowers can you find? - 10 points for each type spotted.

10) Follow the path along, ignoring any paths on the left or right.

This varied woodland is great for minibeasts. - 10 points for each species spotted.

Woodlouse

Good minibeasts area

There are three carved signs on this section. Write the names here.

11) When you reach a track with a house on your right, turn to the left.

Total points

38

12) Walk past the pub to reach the road.

13) Cross the road and take the path opposite to walk up the hill.

Can you find any evidence of deer? e.g. flattened areas of bracken or tracks like these - 20 points for any evidence you can find.

There are three carved signs along this section. Write the names here.
(Check your answers below - 5 points for each one you find)

Can you find evidence of deer?

14) At the top of the hill, follow the path round to the right past a picnic table.

15) Passing some bike trails on your right, you will reach an area in the woods where several paths meet. Follow the path round to the left.

The Rose and Crown

16) Upon reaching the road, turn left to walk a short distance to the crossroads. Find a path opposite to lead you back to the car park.

Total points

Carved signposts - Fly agaric, beech, badger, scots pine, birch, rowan, fox, holly and ivy, sweet chestnut, tawny owl, heather, oak.

More Wild Places

There are many more wild places to explore throughout Kent and here are just a few our favourite suggestions.

1) Kearsney Abbey Gardens and Russell Gardens.

Located on the Alkham Valley road near to Dover, the Abbey gardens have a fascinating variety of unusual trees and there are excellent spots for pond and stream dipping.

www.doverdc.co.uk

2) Samphire Hoe.

Reclaimed land produced from the spoil heaps from the channel tunnel. Located beneath the white cliffs, it has ponds, peregrine falcons and orchids.

www.samphirehoe.com

3) Fowlmead Country Park (Sandwich area).

Recently created nature reserve with water fowl and nature trail.

www.fowlmead.co.uk/nature2

4) Monkton Nature Reserve (Thanet).

This reserve is set in 16 acres of an abandoned chalk quarry. It houses the Thanet observatory and the first artificial bat cave in the country.

www.mnr.manston.net

5) Pegwell Bay Nature Reserve.

Rock pools, cliffs, caves and mud flats with internationally important bird populations such as curlew, redshank and ringed plovers.

www.vistithanet.co.uk

More Wild Places

6) Thorden Wood, Clowes Wood and Blean Woods (Canterbury and Whitstable area).

One of the largest areas of broadleaved woodland in southern britain. A site for the rare Heath Fritillary butterfly and Nightingales can be found here.

www.theblean.co.uk

7) Stodmarsh Nature Reserve (Canterbury area).

Bird hides are in place to watch water fowl on the rivers, marshes and meadows.

www.kentishstour.org.uk

8) Denge Woods (near Petham).

Famous for its rare orchids and flowers, especially in the spring. It is dominated by sweet chestnut coppice alongside an area of former chalk grassland.

www.woodlandtrust.org.uk

9) Kings Wood (Chilham).

A very large ancient wood with sculpture trail, children's play area (with a number of unusual play structures created to represent creatures in the forest).

www.friendsofkingswood.org

10) The Elham Valley Walk.

A long distance walk from Canterbury to Folkstone that has many interesting sections for wildlife along the route.

Guide book - Elham Valley Way by Brian Hart and Ella Lawton

Paying attractions

11) Howletts Wild Animal Park.

Famous for its colony of gorillas, discover wildlife from around the world.

www.howletts.com

12) The Wildwood Trust (Herne).

A conservation centre with a variety of native and non-native species.

www.wildwoodtrust.org

Wild About the Coast

There are many great places to explore around the coast.
- here are some of our favourite suggestions.

2) Romans at Reculver
- visit the towers and country park to discover more about the plants, birds and insects along this stretch of coast.

Isle of Sheppey

Herne Bay

Whitstable

1) Shells and seabirds at Seasalter

- Once a centre for salt production, this area of extensive mudflats and marshes is great for birdlife and the beach is full of shells.

4) Liners, a lighthouse and lizards at Langdon Cliffs
- Starting at the Langdon Cliffs National Trust car park take the cliff top path towards St Margaret's Bay. Pass the docks below to eventually reach the South Foreland Lighthouse. Continue along to reach St Margaret's Bay. Along the cliffs, look for Exmoor Ponies, butterflies, peregrine falcons and Lizards.

Red Admiral

Shore crab

3) Smugglers, sand dunes and seaweed
- When the tide is low, start by the minigolf course at Cliftonville and go down to the beach at Walpole Bay. Walk along the beach around the North Foreland to Palm Bay, Botany Bay, Kingsgate Bay and Joss Bay. You should be able to spot the caves previously used by smugglers and there are rock pools and sand dunes to explore all the way along.
If the tide is high, you can take the path along the cliff tops instead.

Margate
North Foreland
Pegwell Bay
Deal
St Margaret's Bay
Dover

Become an expert beachcomber and look carefully along the tide line for all sorts of flotsam and jetsam.

Wild About East Kent Wordsearch

A	Q	R	F	D	G	H	A	W	T	H	O	R	N	X	Z	P	O	M	J
N	H	T	G	V	W	K	L	M	R	A	E	D	E	L	R	T	I	N	P
W	V	H	Y	S	M	L	H	F	L	P	F	W	G	L	L	G	J	R	V
H	K	L	T	E	A	L	P	J	T	V	B	A	Z	Q	D	K	L	U	B
Q	V	F	K	Y	T	F	M	L	I	R	D	V	C	E	S	Y	H	C	F
W	T	I	P	F	B	W	C	O	C	A	T	S	R	F	K	Q	N	O	U
G	B	C	D	E	T	K	N	W	A	N	P	Q	T	D	Y	W	Z	X	V
F	J	L	Y	W	I	H	F	O	P	F	C	U	D	E	L	J	N	L	M
R	L	R	E	D	I	P	S	D	B	V	U	I	T	J	A	K	W	Q	B
D	U	H	K	N	T	O	R	E	C	K	I	R	T	F	R	U	N	H	E
E	R	W	M	N	G	T	D	E	T	O	P	R	D	B	K	M	H	E	D
E	E	P	G	F	E	S	W	L	C	X	J	E	Y	O	L	W	R	M	E
W	T	M	P	F	D	R	A	G	O	N	F	L	Y	W	I	C	O	H	P
K	S	X	F	T	U	J	N	L	D	U	T	I	Y	W	H	S	A	K	I
W	Y	F	B	C	I	T	H	F	K	L	S	E	D	K	L	T	G	S	T
A	O	P	T	G	R	E	V	H	M	B	L	E	R	F	H	O	D	C	N
H	R	J	U	G	S	A	Q	P	L	B	N	F	V	D	E	W	I	B	E
H	V	S	Y	C	A	M	O	R	E	R	E	W	K	L	G	F	C	X	C
R	I	P	G	F	R	E	D	B	V	C	N	L	G	R	D	L	Y	V	E
N	M	I	Y	R	D	C	F	V	G	N	W	O	O	D	L	O	U	S	E

Can you spot these ten different species of Kent wildlife in the grid above?

TEAL   SYCAMORE   DRAGONFLY   CENTIPEDE

SKYLARK   WOODLOUSE

HAWTHORN   SPIDER   OYSTER   SQUIRREL

So how did you score on the walk ?

Over 250 points - seriously wild! - excellent spotting.
160 - 250 points - wild potential - welldone.
50 - 150 points - rather tame - time to become more wild!

Remember to revisit at another time of year to try to beat your previous score.